# IMMIGRATION
# EMIGRATION
# DIVERSITY

# IMMIGRATION
# EMIGRATION
# DIVERSITY
## AN ANTHOLOGY

TIMOTHY F. CROWLEY

AND

JAKI SHELTON GREEN

CHAPEL HILL
PRESS, INC.

COVER IMAGE: About 180 Million years ago, the super continent, Pangaea began to break up, continuing to move to this day, following the convection currents, and along with it, every living being moving with the ebb and flow of the energy of the Universe.

Excerpt from *The Prophet* by Kahlil Gibran, © 1923 by Kahlil Gibran and renewed 1951 by Administrators C.T.A. of Kahlil Gibran Estate and Mary G. Gibran. Used by permission of Alfred A. Knopf, a division of Random House, Inc.

"To a Stranger Born in Some Distant Country Hundreds of Years from Now" is from *Picnic, Lightning*, by Billy Collins, © 1998. Reprinted by permission of the University of Pittsburgh Press.

"Who Am I, without Exile?" is from *Unfortunately, It was Paradise*, by Mahmoud Darwish, © 2002 The Regents of the University of California Press. Reprinted by permission of the University of California Press.

"Learning English" © 2000, by Mark Smith-Soto is from *Green Mango Collage*, published by Persephone Press. Reprinted by permission of the author, Mark Smith-Soto.

"How Light the Severed Head" first appeared in *Foliate Oak*.

"Refugee" first appeared in *Red River Review*.

"The Lithuanians" is reprinted from *Prairie Schooner*, volume 78, number 1(Spring 2004), by permission of the University of Nebraska Press. Copyright by the University of Nebraska Press.

"This Is How" also appears in *Rock & Sling*.

Copyright © 2006 Timothy F. Crowley and Jaki Shelton Green

All rights reserved. No part of this book may be used, reproduced or transmitted in any form or by any means, electronic or mechanical, including photograph, recording, or any information storage or retrieval system, without the express written permission of the copyright holder, except where permitted by law.

ISBN 1-59715-003-7
Library of Congress Catalog Number 2005921033

Printed in the United States of America
First Printing

This anthology is dedicated to countless generations of daughters and sons, survivors of the journey of immigration and emigration.

The book is a timeless testimony to the possibilities of new hope, new visions and new graces that only the ultimate immigrants, our children and their children, can bring forth and foster through the celebration of diversity.

These words from *The Prophet*, by Kahlil Gibran, bear witness to and validate the voices and music of our ancestors:

Your children are not your children.
They are the sons and daughters of life's
longing for itself.

For their souls dwell in the house of tomorrow,
which you cannot visit, not even in your
dreams.

You are the bows from which your children,
as living arrows, are sent forth.

For even as he loves the arrow that flies,
so He loves the bow that is stable.

KAHLIL GIBRAN

*Timothy F. Crowley and Jaki Shelton Green*

# Table of Contents

Acknowledgements  *ix*

Spirit Sister ~ Timothy F. Crowley  *2*
Spirit Sister Listening ~ Jaki Shelton Green  *4*
To A Stranger Born In Some Distant
  Country Hundreds of Years from Now ~ Billy Collins  *6*
Immigration Trifold ~ Timothy F. Crowley  *8*
Boat People ~ Hoang-Anh L. Tran  *9*
Mai: Three Definitions ~ Hoang-Anh L. Tran  *10*
As A Woman ~ Donna McAdoo Jones  *11*
Refugee ~ Joanna C. Scott  *12*
America *Is* an Immigrant Experience ~ Lynn Veach Sadler  *15*
Excerpt from *The Prophet* ~ Kahlil Gibran  *17*
Chicago "El" ~ Gwen Y. Fortune  *19*
The Loss Of The Emigrants ~ John Boyle O'Reilly  *20*
Inmates Working ~ Timothy F. Crowley  *22*
The Black Lacquered Box ~ Margaret Boothe Baddour  *24*
Ellas ~ Catherine Combs  *26*
Cousin Awa ~ Timothy F. Crowley  *28*
Aunt Kate ~ A. Conrad Neuman  *30*
Black Ice ~ Kate McCabe  *33*
Che Guevera ~ McCabe Coolidge  *36*
Sugar Cane ~ Jennifer S. Madriaga  *40*
My Mother's Uncle John ~ Luba V. Zakharov  *43*
World View ~ Timothy F. Crowley  *47*
Exile ~ Joanna A. McKethan  *48*

The German Doctor ~ Maureen Sherbondy  51
Pursuing Freedom ~ Brenda Kay Ledford  53
Changes ~ Timothy F. Crowley  54
At Ellis Island ~ David Radavich  55
Tuesday Woman ~ Ruth Winchester Ware  59
Two ways To Leave Home ~ Betsy Humphreys  60
Wait ~ Patricia Barber  62
How Light, the Severed Head ~ E. V. Noechel  64
Learning English/Lección de inglés ~ Mark Smith-Soto  65
Ancestors ~ Joy Acey  66
How Tall Is Your Boy ~ Joy Acey  68
The Naming ~ Bonnie Michael  69
The Lithuanians ~ Andrea Selch  71
Untitled ~ Will Whitaker  74
Angel Baby Heaven ~ C. Pleasants York  75
Little Bird ~ Martha Klopfer  76
Louise ~ William Menza  78
Ode To Horace Mann ~ Doug Stuber  82
Pink Chang ~ Doug Stuber  83
An Alien Dream ~ Emmanuel K. Ngwainmbi  84
This Is How ~ Fred Bahnson  86
Ode To An Abandoned Name ~ Jeanette Cabanis-Brewin  88
A Ransom Of Bones ~ Jaki Shelton Green  90
Who Am I, without Exile? ~ Mahmoud Darwish  98

# Acknowledgements

The majority of the poems so generously contributed to this collection have been chosen from many extremely powerful pieces of verse submitted during a two-year period of time.

Along with great appreciation for the publishing firms and estates of certain prominent poets known on an international level, who granted permission to reprint their works in this anthology, we wish to thank the following poets who understand the power of verse and its application to the subject matter of this anthology, *Immigration, Emigration, and Diversity*.

Joy Acey
Margaret Boothe Baddour
Fred Bahnson
Patricia Barber
Jeanette Cabanis-Brewin
Catherine Combs
McCabe Coolidge
Gwen Y. Fortune
Betsy Humphreys
Donna McAdoo Jones
Martha Klopfer
Brenda Kay Ledford
Jennifer S. Madriaga
Kate McCabe
Joanna A. McKethan
William Menza

Bonnie Michael
A. Conrad Neuman
Emmanuel K. Ngwainmbi
E. V. Noechel
David Radavich
Lynn Veach Sadler
Joanna C. Scott
Andrea Selch
Maureen Sherbondy
Doug Stuber
Hoang-Anh L. Tran
Ruth Winchester Ware
Will Whitaker
C. Pleasants York
Luba V. Zakharov

Once more, we thank those poets who have given of themselves without compromise and who openly share a need to better understand all inhabitants of this Mother Earth.

All earnings from this effort are deposited in the www.writersforpeace.org fund and used to finance any future events associated with www.writersforpeace.org.

Sincerely,
Timothy F. Crowley
Jaki Shelton Green
*Fellow poets/editors*

# RACISM
## IS IT MORE THAN SKIN DEEP?

### ...bus sailed ...h baggage

...scribe to their world-view.
Another eerie counterpoint to recent Islamic extremist behavior was an incident during the Battle of Lepanto in 1571. The combined naval forces of the Pope, Spain and Venice crushed the fleet of the Turkish Ottoman Empire... capturing the Christian... and ship, the... the mast of... tributed...

F. POWERS
Were it not for ... would not

### ...g party beaten in Hong Kong

...have some staying power... believe the government got... " said Yeung Sum,... the Democrats. His expectations even... were ostensibly such as san-... loftier ideals... ge being...

many called a threat to civil liberties was a turning point in Hong Kong politics. It forced Tung to shelve the bill in his first big retreat since he took office when Britain returned Hong Kong to China in 1997. Tung's opponents began clamoring loudly for full democracy in...

a climate further charged weak economy.
The DAB's poor showing... seen as a backlash again... It raised the stakes for elections next... pro-democra... to gain...

ism Network in Durham. Much of h... had driven [to a restaura... tting ready t...

### ...ejudice as a mental disor...

N F. POUSSAINT

**BOSTON**

Can it be sickness that makes people hate...

...are loath to label ...reme racist behavior ...l illness. Consider the ...ce the arrest of ...rrow Jr., who admit-... rampage in Los ...ths after the ...tal health system

...tive of King County ...cial in the Seattle ...'s arrest: "People ...se that this ki...

rather than an indication of... pathology.
In addition, the as... racism a mental... absolute raci... ity, thus... self...

### Boston's Racial Barriers Slow to Fall

#### Bus Error Evokes Old Divisions

By JONATHAN FINER
Washington Post Staff Writer

WELLESLEY, Mass.—At the end of the first day of school, a confused kindergartner from this affluent suburb west of Boston was guided by a confused teacher onto the wrong bus. It carried him to Dorchester, an urban borough south of downtown.

A simple mistake, perhaps, and thanks to a vigilant parent at the other end of the line, the boy was quickly returned home, none the worse for wear.

But in a region that still hears the story of attempts to forcibly desegregate Boston's schools almost 30 years ago, the incident—in which a white teacher assumed that a black child was part of a program that shuttles inner-city minority students to... white suburban schools—reopened old wounds... availed an investigation in... racial lines played a...

#### Lacking Diversity

In the Boston area, only a quarter of all blacks and Hispanics live in the suburbs. Nationwide, the proportion is much higher.

Percentage of racial group that lives in the suburbs

In the greater Boston area
- White: 73%
- Asian: 48%
- Hispanic: 25%
- Black: 22%

In the U.S.
- White: 71%
- Asian: 58%
- Hispanic: 49%
- Black: 35%

...cy of the bruising busing experiment of the 1970s is a program called Metco, a less controversial attempt at desegregation. The flow of students goes in only one direction, with minority students being bused to the suburbs. Some 3,000 of Boston's 62,000 public school students participate, Payzant said.

About 150 are bused back and forth every day to Wellesley, a leafy college town where minorities make up less than 10 percent of the population and where slightly more than 400 of the 28,000 residents are black. One of the wealthiest and whitest communities in the Boston area, Wellesley is no stranger to high-profile incidents of racial prejudice. In 1990 a black resident and star guard for the Boston Celtics basketball team, Dee Brown, was stopped in his car, made to lie face down on the pavement and arrested by police who concluded without much evidence that he had robbed a nearby bank.

That incident led to the firing of the town's police chief and to some local soul-searching on the consequences... said Richard McGhee, who in the weeks following Brown's arrest founded the World of Wellesley, a group that promotes multicultural... awareness in town through lec... tors and school programs...

McGhee said he saw the following recent bus error as a... need to hear about the...

...own the town...
A major consequence of sentiments like these, minority leaders in the Boston area say, is that the city has long found it difficult to attract and retain minority professionals who would prefer not to live downtown but don't feel comfortable in homogeneous suburbs. While overt instances of racism are less common, they are not unheard of.

Just last month, a wealthy white Boston suburb refused to pay an aerospace engineer $50,000 for rejecting his application after finding out he was black. Steve Johnson came to Boston with his wife and two children from a Chicago suburb in 2000... iting profes... setts Institu...

The landlord...
estate agen...
would be...
to a black...
Makin...
ble to... a may...
ton Co...
Jim...
exe...
20...
B...

pent of blacks and Hispanics live in suburbs. In the Boston area, that number is less than 25 percent, according to the report, written by John Logan, director... Lewis Mumford Center... Albany, the State Uni...

## Spirit Sister

Layers of synthetic light
radiate evening's obscurity....
The womb of many waters
contains its secrets
from where we embark,
transcending this mystery.....

The world awaits
this courted being...
continuing its aggressive instincts:
antithesis of peace,
bearer of negligent chemistry...

Layers of humanity
depend and refer to
this impending glorious
calamity....

Spirit sister
I reach out to you,
searching for guidance, trust,
continuity....

Layers of water work their way
through mountain streams,
boundlessness washing away
suppressed whim, unfulfilled desire,
reproductive incompetence,
foolish fancy...

Courage…courage to risk the
climb beneath these generational layers,
seeking an alternative energy:
a balance against the ragged edge,
fearful coexistence..

Layers of skin
defined by melanin.
its purposeful demeaning
of ancestral reference
all in the guise of spirituality…

Violence, perpetual combat
sponsored by sport and greed,
calling to the NAME in vain,
sacrificing integrity.…

Spirit Sister, my Spirit Sister
reach out to me!!

TIMOTHY F. CROWLEY

## spirit sister listening

what does the night think of the poet
sitting in her chair
pretending to know the language of
darkness
what does the night think of the words I use
to scatter stars off the path
of a slave woman
who prays that the moon
will oversleep
and not trace
her footsteps.
what does the night think of the poet
black
stealing
the winding shawl of hours
crawling across a headless sky.
we are wombs
the night and i
i am this poet.
sitting.
listening.
at night she would whisper,
"i can hear the sea. the ground, the sky counting
children
mothers
fathers
counting
names."

my grandmother held the stories
of her grandmother carefully
inside connected stitches
these are her words,
"i can hear the ground counting…."
patterns shapes colors
rise from the water
she collects the sands of lives she cannot name
hush
hush
the river is counting the names
rivers she cannot name
but the waters are one she sings
gathering together
sifting bones
sifting bones
sifting bones.
on the beach I walk carefully
listening
stealing these bones
that sing.


JAKI SHELTON GREEN

# To A Stranger Born in Some Distant Country Hundreds of Years from Now

*"I write poems for a stranger who will be born in some distant country hundreds of years from now."* MARY OLIVER

Nobody here likes a wet dog.
No one wants anything to do with a dog
that is wet from being out in the rain
or retrieving a stick from a lake.
Look how she wanders around the crowded pub tonight
going from one person to another
hoping for a pat on the head, a rub behind the ears,
something that could be given with one hand
without even wrinkling the conversation.

But everyone pushes her away,
some with a knee, others with the sole of a boot.
Even the children, who don't realize she is wet
until they go to pet her,
push her away
then wipe their hands on their clothes.
And whenever she heads toward me,
I show her my palm, and she turns aside.

O stranger of the future!
O inconceivable being!
whatever the shape of your house,
however you scoot from place to place,
no matter how strange and colorless the clothes you may wear,
I bet nobody there likes a wet dog either.
I bet everybody in your pub,
even the children, pushes her away.


BILLY COLLINS

## Immigration Trifold

⁓ Fuchsia flowered One,
stoking tearful, hissing,
earthly, farewell embers.
Embarking on a "coffin ship"
as morning light appears,
parents slip back into
twelve milkers....

Childrens', childrens', childrens' children
borne into a blissful, enlightened
social grace.

Ominous oceans carry heirs.
human spirit spills into
overflowing water basins.
Life's source subsists
as oppression exists,
while the morning light of courage
of all humanity persists
persists, persists...

TIMOTHY F. CROWLEY

## Boat People:

specks suspended between
seastorms and charred death.
In war, they do not escape
leaving with the others scrambling
from rooftops to the whopwhopwhop
slicing the sky into fragments.
Instead, they cling to fishing boats,
linking arms to fence out the sea's rage.
Some wear no rings—a glint sold
for the space of a dream, bags
barely roped to the edge of a boat.
They remember soldier-
boys mirrored in family
albums burned to a yellow crisp
of setting suns; at night
they steer with their breath
clamped in silence, riding the crests
under the pinprick eyes of God.

HOANG – ANH L. TRAN

# Mai: Three Definitions

In second grade,
I learned *mai*: a flower
I thought it meant:
mother, mẹ—a nod, a resignation.
Reticence humming in
the force of another sound.
But I was wrong.

The weight of three letters:
yellow petals open
in the pages of a book, praying.
In Vietnamese, it means:
tomorrow. Perhaps *mai* is:
to sew, sharp tips piercing together.
It is a name given and worn
like a necklace. Not dropped
between pauses,
it is a sound: After the slap, a kiss.
No, it is the voice of wind
outside thin glass, sighing *Mai*.

HOANG-ANH L. TRAN

## As A Woman

I will claim my dignity
with a grace that only I can,
reflected by my stride
stepping forth
refusing to shrink
or walk as though I've harmed anyone.
the light of me continues to shine
as I declare the glow of my truth,
which continues to sparkle
and reflect the beauty
of my sassiness and my style.
my smile continues
uplifted by honor.
my laughter,
a celebration of spirit
the sheer delight of me,
transcends small things and small minds
with a joy that sustains me
as a woman.

DONNA McADOO JONES

# Refugee

*(Philippine Refugee Processing Center, Bataan, 1985, since destroyed in the eruption of Mt. Pinatubo)…for Roel, my driver*

He would squat in the shade
All day beside a hulk
Hoisted off some beach
Where boat people had run
Aground. Brushing away
Children from the local
Village come to beg, he
Would gossip with a Khmer,
Or Lao, or Vietnamese.
While I did my research
With tapes and interviews,
He did his own less formal
Kind. Sly inquisitor,
He led his subject on
With simple English
Sentences, a smiling
Dumb-show for the rest,
Talking of unimportant
Things at first, thus drawing
Out more serious concerns.

Later he would tell me
Of this one or that who had
Come to pass the time
With him, telling a tale
Of dark beach rendezvous,

Gold passing hand to hand,
Fear, hunger, pirates, storms,
Relief of gaining land.
One man told of giant
Fish with giant fins who
Rode beside their boat like
Guardian ancestors.
Another said a gull
Soared in the wind before
Their boat thirteen full
Days, guiding them to shore.
Now he came each morning
With bags of rice and crumbs
To feed the gulls here in
The main square of the camp.

Meeting me one evening
With the car, Roel seemed down.
"What's up?" He sighed.
"Ma'am, these are lucky ones.
America to them
says, '*Come.*' To us, so poor,
it shakes its head.
Even, Ma'am, the children
From Morong, my mother's
village, come here every
Day to beg for rice and
Pesos from these refugees.

Oh Ma'am, if only I…"
I winced, held out my hand.
"Roel, please don't. Don't cry."
But now here came the beggar
Children shouting down
The track. He slid apologetic
Eyes away and turned
A stiff, disowning back.


JOANNA C. SCOTT

# America *Is* an Immigrant Experience

In the Greenwich National Maritime Museum,
time suspends.
Lionel Wyllie's emigrants
approach New York,
hearts in throats, breaths held.
Steerage must wait
for the First and Second Class
to disembark at Ellis Island.
Steerage toilets were
for "Male" and "Female";
First Class demarked
"Gentlemen" and "Ladies,"
though the money of the cruise lines
was made upon the steerage.

In between wars,
fleeing economic depression,
they come in hope.
They come in thousands—
from Britain and from Europe—
from the end of the Napoleonic War
until the opening of World War I.
They come in thousands—
potato famine driving
exodus from Ireland.

The Immigrant Sea opens
America to receive them.
They will be its Nile Delta,
its Fertile Crescent.
They come, come in thousands,
each with a thousand dreams,
each with ten thousand hopes.

In the Greenwich National Maritime Museum,
time suspends.
A United Colors of Benetton poster,
photograph of Oliviero Tosrani,
offers Albanian refugees,
arriving at Bari, Italy.
A stopgap merely?

In America, time suspends.
Hearts in throats,
breaths held,
we Americans *are* our past.

LYNN VEACH SADLER

# Excerpt from *The Prophet*

And a woman who held a babe against her bosom said,
Speak to us of Children.
And he said:
Your children are not your children.
They are the sons and daughters of Life's longing for itself.
They come through you but not from you,
And though they are with you,
yet they belong not to you.
You may give them your love but not your thoughts.
For they have their own thoughts.
You may house their bodies but not their souls,
For their souls dwell in the house of tomorrow, which you cannot visit, not even in your dreams.
You may strive to be like them,
but seek not to make them like you.
For life goes not backward nor tarries with yesterday.
You are the bows from which your children as living arrows are sent forth.
The archer sees the mark upon the path of the infinite,

and He bends you with His might that
His arrows may go swift and far.
Let your bending in the archer's hand be for gladness;
For even as he loves the arrow that flies,
so He also loves the bow that is stable.

KAHLIL GIBRAN

# Chicago "El"

Screaming curses, the elevated train grinds.
Sand scratched windows, frame crumbling
dames of Victorian grandeur,
not yet gentrified;
avenues wash
a grunge of paper,
plastic, and urban loss.

Lakefront condos, immigrant enclaves,
Thai, Humoung—names that lie strangely
on American tongues.
Two brown boys on a freshly painted stoop,
their hair magenta spikes,
smile, smoke waffling,
into a forbidden magazine.

Grey tinged snow, snagged curtains, half-mast,
a spotted puppy, bulging with a recent meal,
bright-cheeked girls, a blonde, a brunette
chew sugar sprinkled doughnuts
and swing a crystal on a string.
The elevated blurs
red-spayed graffiti:
    Han Keno
    loves
    Monisha Jones

GWEN Y. FORTUNE

# The Loss of the Emigrants.

*The Steamer "Atlantic" Was Wrecked Near Halifax, N. S., April 1, 1878, And 560 Lives Lost.*

For months and years, with penury and want
And heart-sore envy did they dare to cope,
And mite by mite was saved from earnings scant,
To buy, some future day, the God-sent hope.

They trod the crowded streets of hoary towns,
Or tilled from year to year the wearied fields,
And in shadow of the golden crowns,
They gasped for sunshine and the health it yields.

They turned from homes all cheerless, child and man,
With kindly feelings only for the soil,
And for the kindred faces, pinched and wan,
That prayed and stayed, unwillingly, at their toil.

They lifted up their faces to the Lord,
And read His answer in the westering sun,
That called them ever as a shining word,
And beckoned seawards the rivers run.

They looked their last, wet-eyed, on Swedish hills,
On German villages, and English dales;
Like brooks that grow from many mountain rills,
The peasant-stream flowed out from Irish vales.

Their grief at parting was not all a grief
But blended sweetly with the joy to come.
When from full store they spared the rich relief
To gladden all the dear ones left at home.

"We thank thee, God!" they cried; "The cruel gate
That barred our lives has swung beneath Thy hand;
Behind our ship now frowns the cruel fate,
Before her smiles the teeming Promised Land!"

Alas! when shown in mercy or in wrath,
How weak we are to read God's awful lore!
His breath protected on the stormy path
And dashed them lifeless on the promised shore!

His hand sustained them in the parting woe,
And gave bright vision to the heart of each.
His waters bore them where they wished to go,
Then swept them seaward from the very beach!

Their home is reached; their fetters now are riven.
Their humble toil is o'er; their rest has come.
A land was promised, and a land was given.
But, oh! God help the waiting ones at home!

JOHN BOYLE O'REILLY

## Inmates Working

Observing, understanding
freedom's illusion
by the side of the highway,
shaded from the scorching sun,
silent, endless lob lolly pines
beyond barb wire,
electrified fence, motion detectors,
and technically perfect back-up resources.

Our children, pieces of several
million, locked into an industry
overseen by emaciated beaked-hat
bearing, mustached stereotype,
degrees removed
from the guarded
with antiquated firearm…
skull and bones
etched on forearm…
Surreal.

Only accident of birth
enables us the opportunity
to avoid this Way Without Liberty.
Ready at a moment's notice
to discharge at fast feet fleeing
or any attempt to disarm.

Dead on or destroying
another body part,
reacting to morning's
altercation with boss, spouse, lover,
another…

Our babies, without defense,
without sense, all spent
for free labor, under justice for all.
With message missent,
powerless against
Energy supported by
sub industries of black gold,
government approved drugs.
National defense—compassionless.

TIMOTHY F. CROWLEY

# The Black Lacquered Box
— *Molodova 2003*

### I. At the Fantaze Shop

On the black lacquered box, a butterfly
hovers over orange tiger lilies.
One carved, yellow-flecked wing juts out.
The tourists pick it up and lay it down.
Open here in my palm, the red inside
dazzles me. I must have this box.
In her red and black embroidered blouse
the shopkeeper frowns, her round cheeks,
full lips marked by the Ottoman Empire.
She turns over the box and says, "300 lei,"
eyebrows raised. I add it to my pile
of stacking dolls, woven belts, painted eggs.
"Da," I smile at her, "300 lei."

II.  At the Ministry of Defense

Back and forth fly the words. I almost nod
off as the Labor Minister's words roll
on and on, and the interpreter's sharp
English punctuates his Romanian lilt.
His Russian face is long and angular.
"What can you do," he asks again, "to help?
Invest in our country, our industries."
I jolt awake as he says, "300 lei—
is the new minimum wage." Per hour?
Per week? "No, no—is minimum per month."
In my suitcase, the frivolous butterfly
beats her wings. I must have this box.
I need this box—to remember Molodova.

MARGARET BOOTHE BADDOUR

## Ellas

Dropping a dark litter alongside the gutter,
to organize the menial tasks of others:
the picking up
the putting away
the straightening up
of stuff and more stuff…
belching fumes, the CAT lumbers on.

Up pops a carnival of nylon fuchsias, lemon-limes,
aquamarines
pulled tight over fragile ribs of respite shade.
Spinning espadrilles of crisscrossing pairs
rise hot over sticky asphalt in the morning sun.
Turning a dark cheek to the mist,
they reggae on into the suburban framework.

CATHERINE COMBS

## Cousin Awa

Awa bids good morning
and addresses me "percentage man."
I dig in for my early
morning coffee change.
Alone by the extravagant indoor waterfall,
created within the belly
of International Place,
adjacent to the World Bank,
secured by a cast of thousands.
Such subtle power!

How she knows who, why,
or what I am?
She smiles a sweetness—
a Third World kind.
I know that smile.
I have encountered it
often on vacation.
That almost purple skin
belies all innocence and
a troubled mind.

I dare to consider she knows
all about me from CNN
and my insatiable need
for instant gratification
of material goods, living
off her family's backs,
"back home."

She, Awa, has found her way here,
searching for some sort of liberty.
Where other than Washington D.C.?
I salute her and
address her dark brown—
eyed genetic map of
unbearable hurt
and courage…

Indeed I work for a percentage.
My most recent model auto
is parked for nineteen dollars
per day—possibly twenty-five…
She sends that amount
home weekly,
so her family and family's family
may barely survive.

Oh, she'll find her way.
"They" always do. Just
as our ancestors worked
their joy and their
tears of sorrow
with the music of birth.
I know Awa well!..

TIMOTHY F. CROWLEY

## Aunt Kate

Aunt Kate, crumb cake.
Soups that take all day to make.
Her hair piled on top in a large gray bun,
Her chair along side the kitchen table
Where she sat and stared at the coal stove
When her chores were done.
Soon she'd go painful to the cellar bin
For another hod of coal,
Riddle the grate and toss it in.
Then sit and wait for Aunt Gert
To come home from her job at the hospital
Or from a night at the Eastern Star.
Aunt Kate kept company
With only the coal stove, Aunt Gert, and God.

She came from the Old Country
Before the Great War,
With Opa. Oma, my father, and Aunt Gert,
They lived in Hell's Kitchen for a time,
Until Opa got well-to-do enough to move
To Bayside with the business.
Aunt Kate was really Kate Koch, the cook
When the family was rich in the Rhineland,
Before Opa ran afoul of the Kaiser,
And they left Frankfort on the run.
Opa lost the business in the depression,
And soon after, Opa and Oma died.
Aunt Gert went to work,
And Aunt Kate stayed home

In the big house in Bayside
With the life-sized figures of the saints
On the wallpaper in the dim dining room.
She lived out her life in the kitchen
With the big coal stove,
The spooner full of spoons,
And the cleanest kitchen floor
On two Sixteenth Street.
There wasn't even a cat.

When we came to live for awhile,
So I could go to school,
She took me on like the coal stove,
Shook me down and saw I was fed.
I was her friend then, not a pretend son.
She'd treat my adolescent anxieties
with crumb cake and soup
And some Teutonic words of advice,
Always said with a wink and a nudge.
It was important to her that I did well in school.
She could get very serious about that.
"Study hard, youse'll loin!" She'd admonish
With a wag of an arthritic finger
And the clacking of teeth.

I remember the day the principal
Called me into his office
And Uncomfortably informed me that
Aunt Kate had died suddenly at home.

He told me I was excused for the day
And was surprised I declined.
Better I stay and study hard and learn.
She'd prefer that.
I can give her that,
That which she gave me,
Something solid, like determination.

Aunt Kate, Kate Koch,
The cook from the Old Country.
She loved me, I guess.
I sure loved her
And her spätzles.


A. CONRAD NEUMAN

# Black Ice

The weather channel
shows an ice-breaker
ploughing the frozen Hudson River,
its sharp bow opening a channel
for the oil tankers
hauling the black gold
of winter into the harbor.

Then the scene switches
to the frozen Schuylkill River
in Philadelphia,
just beyond the art museum,
where the lone silhouette
of a woman in a long coat,
black-gloved hand
holding a scarf
across her mouth
against the smoking air,
is skating silently
on the smooth, vacant ice.

After threading
the stiff laces
of her skates, which
walking along the river
before work,
she may have left on the porch
of one of the empty boat houses,
she glides out across
the black, silken ice,
quiet,
solitary,
absorbed.

Top of the local news hour,
at the port of Norfolk,
a man in Marine fatigues,
who leaves a new wife behind
in Philadelphia,
the news reporter learns,
re-laces up one of his
high, black boots,
then adjusts the camouflage hat
that's meant to hide him
from silver missiles
shaped like flying icicles.

His ship,
on stand-by,
will be pulling out
soon,
he's not sure when,
ploughing its way
through the glacial waves
of the vast, black ocean,
to a place he's not
meant to know,
for security reasons,
somewhere beyond
the Cape of Good Hope
that lies directly adjacent
to False Bay.


KATE McCABE

## Che Guevera

Che Guevera walked into town today.
He flew out the next, mangled body
tied to the bottom of a helicopter.
He came to town tired, winded, looking
for comrades, Speaking Spanish
he appeared briefly in the plaza.
My neighbors speak Quechua or Ayamara and some Spanish.
Did they need him, this Cuban revolutionary,
These urban campesinos working the mines for a dime a day?
Maybe Che needed them. More than he knew. Than they knew.
He, out of breath, out of time, and out of life
lingered too long.
"Hide out Che!" I would have yelled out
across the plaza, "Go to where your brothers are!"
Descend, into that hell.
Silver, gone, shipped to Spain.
Remnants of tin, that's what left.
But you knew that didn't you Che?
The mine only takes, doesn't give back.
These urban Quechua speaking fathers die
when their 30$^{th}$ birthday rolls around.
Like you, they are gasping, but they
don't know, unlike you, what is
killing them. They are haunted.
No word for silicosis nor black lung.
No health insurance, Their comrades
and brothers die. The next day I welcome their children.
Into the "hogar." The home for miners' kids.

You are hunted. Haunted too?
What is your connection to them?
What's behind the fire in your eyes?
Tell us!

Both of you die today.
You and the Vision.
This vision of South American revolution
does not go full circle.
Your death takes away
its first crack at life.
Stand in line. Che.
Your lofty phrases
here in the mountains
at 12,000 feet,
found no perch no catchbasin.
Like ashes now, floating,
just floating, aspiring fragments.
Like you, too late,
with no homebase.

"Comrades, brothers,"
You said. But you missed them.
Only students and taxi cab drivers in that plaza.
You missed them, standing on that platform,
they were down below,
chewing cocoa leaves. Lunch.
Cool, moist cave like mine.

Comrades and brothers, pausing
for breath, for a little euphoria.
Each day they go down,
until breath runs out,
or the canary dies. Either way
Che, you missed out.
Broken connection. Until the end.
Until the end of your day. This day.
The day your breath ran out.
Like them you were lifted up.
Taken away. But they didn't
know you, didn't miss you.
Broken connection No circle..

I knew you were in town.
The older boys told me.
These orphan boys. They knew the scoop.
They knew you were here.
But they said to me, "demasiado tarde."
Too late for their fathers.
Too late for them. Oh
yes, they were learning Spanish,
but they want me to teach them
English.

Escape clause, out of the mine.
They don't want to go with me
tonight to the plaza.
University students said,
"Bring a candle." But my
boys say, "Do these students
light a candle for our papas?"
Who was Che anyway?
"Demasiado tarde." For him, for us.
These orphan boys heads' have already turned
away from the Plaza, from Cuba.
They turn toward me:
"Senior Willy, tell us again how to say
"Los Estados Unidos" in English?

McCABE COOLIDGE

## Sugar Cane

In my dreams,
I am five years old,
My toes in the cool soft dust,
When English is not my first language,
When air smells of
smoked herring and burning wood.

My cousins and I are
behind our house on stilts,
Playing tag behind the stand
where the Pepsi-Cola man
comes to sell in early afternoons

And there is a cat.
It has brown fur,
maybe gray.
And my cousins are saying,
"Pick up the cat. Pick up the cat.
Pick it up by its tail.
It will surely love you then."

I pick up the cat;
It scratches and scratches
at my legs.
But I do not let go.
My cousins laugh.

They say words
that I cannot understand
even in my dreams
Later that day
my *lola* treats my scratches
with merthiolate,
which stings and stains
my skin red.
When the cat comes around
and purrs at *lola*,
she says,
"Bad cat. Bad cat
to hurt my *balasang*."
I hug my *lola*
who is soft and brown
and smells of palm leaves
and coconut oil.

She takes me to market,
and she buys me a piece of
green sugar cane that is
very good to chew and suck on.

When I awaken,
there is more than fifteen years
and ten thousand miles
between us.

It is 10:36 P.M.
in the province of Pangasinan,
and the cooking fires are being put out,
the mosquito nets are being raised,
and my cousins are falling asleep to
the sound of buzzing insects
that fly around in the dark
and glow when you break them open.


JENNIFER S. MADRIAGA

# My Mother's Uncle John

The city crumbles.

Its walls are broken slabs of stone that
split with the slightest touch,
    your fingers
reaching for the latch,
the door,
the gate.
But your reach couldn't hold you up.
    Your body has no form.
It is void of flesh.
    You left it in the rubble
when the city within you fell,
and you crumbled
with its weight upon you
(like your life).
Like the earth
they cover you with—
this land that was never yours.

    You lived a foreigner
in a land that twice was not your own.

    You were lost in your lifetime
in another land
(you spent your lifetime lost).
    Your journey has become
the echo of my story.

       You left it to me,
hidden
in the ark behind the altar of a faith
buried
deep inside my heart,
stirring
to the baritone of your voice
and the gaze of your crooked eyes
that saw the ancient, holy, faith.

      You walked
and wandering out
left your mother Russia,
traveling by night and sleeping by day.
      Your sister tells us you forgot her in the night
and went back to find her sleeping.
Baboonya was with you and the other motley family,
assembled as fearful witness of a hopeful sight,
weighted by the reckless drive to live.

You wanted life.
      You left your home to find it
and left again to save the life you found.

A wandering Aramean was my mother's uncle John:

> he sojourned with few in number and in his land
> cried out to God and the Lord brought them out
> with a mighty hand and outstretched arm
> with great terror, with signs and wonders
> and he brought us into this place and gave us
> this land, a land flowering with milk and honey.*

Every immigrant's story.

They fled,
and now I flee
to the sound of the same call,
the same voice that bore the weight of living
(though lost)
in a land that will never be my own.
    You left it then (and now) so suddenly
that it had no time to welcome
with open gates,
your living soul.

And as time collapses into memory
I see the city crumble;
yet under the weight of the rubble
your soul rises in greeting,
lighting my sadness
at your loss.

You have joined the others
in your land
with the soil
that shapes itself
around my soul,
rounded like your hand
    grasping the standing gate.

LUBA V. ZAKHAROV

*Deuteronomy 26:5–9

# Worldview

That person looks just like me;
not exactly.
His eyes are brown, his hair kinky.
His lips are thick, and his skin has
more melanin;
not exactly.
The nurse is taking from him
what she took from me.
His blood runs red.
That person looks just like me;
exactly!

TIMOTHY F. CROWLEY

# Exile

Native son, who are you?
*A transplant just like me.*
Native son, when may we say,
*This land on which I stand, is home?*

*Who am I?* An American, melted into the USA,
a tile in her mosaic. Indigenous? Not me,
not the Indians, nor descendants of Europe,
the British Isles, Cuba, Russia, Asia, Africa,
or the Iron Curtain Countries. My ancestors
arrived here from foreign shore with a story.

*Who am I?* A Celt who swears she knows Celtic
songs she's never heard before, songs coaxed
from tin whistles and bagpipes. A Scot of rabid
independence and fighting genes. Whose fellow
countrymen were forced from homes by landlords
who practiced land-racking, raising rent so high
they had to leave. They emigrated from beloved
Scotland sometime after the Battle of Culloden.

*Who am I?* A descendent of Scottish highlanders
who found new homes in the dreamy heights
of the Appalachian mountains or in the foothills
near the muddy Cape Fear. For Highlanders,
there *must* be hills near home. There *must* be ballads,
for Scots *must* sing their struggles, their loyalties—
issues of family, love, battles, death, land, and home.

*I am one* who does not take her place for granted.
The new immigrant is my friend. His loyalty has an edge
I cannot match, as though America were a first lover
he could never get over. I traveled to Iron Curtain
countries before the wall came down. I *saw* the tyrant's
captive, heard Jews, Nazi escapees, tell their stories.

I have read *samizdat* on Christians imprisoned
for having Bibles and a faith in Russia, in Romania,
in Hungary, in Czechoslovakia. I have spoken
to friends of those killed for telling political jokes,
killed or exiled to Siberia. The disenfranchised,
the martyrs—the Ivan Moiseyevs tortured for Christian
beliefs—all this *within* their respective native lands.

*Native, I am immigrant still.* Emigrant, immigrant,
exile, sojourner—we tell our forebear's stories. We perch
uneasily in our homes, as if we sat on the cliff edge
of tomorrow, baffled by the news of people dying,
trying to immigrate. We look uneasily at the gift
from the French: Our hostess monument, this
"mother of all exiles," towers over our entrance gate.

*Native, I am exile too*, a stranger, digging foundations
in soil my family has owned for six generations
on the Cape Fear. Yet my husband was called Communist
for studying German. My children were ostracized,

spat on, and despised at school when they returned from life abroad. From my little acres—rivers, ravines, swampland, I face new challenges that want to force me from my place. *I tell you I am an immigrant still.*

Native son, who are you?
*A transplant, just like me.*
Native son, when may we say,
*This land on which we stand, is home?*

JOANNA A. McKETHAN

## The German Doctor

There is a country I have never seen
with its uch's and other guttural
sounds. I try to imagine it,
old buildings, towns, dirt roads
leading to the past. I picture him—
Opa. Juden. Creeping secretly in the black
night, his dark medicine bag in hand—
forbidden journey from patient
to patient. Listening to coughs,
palpating parts, delivering babies
who screamed in the night,
when no one else could or should.

What did it take to lift that visa
from his brother's hand, to leave
a family of wife and kids behind?
What did he abandon
there; did it drift, a flotsam
of guilt, follow him to the port,
to New York? Or, was it left
in concentration camps in the
ashes and piled bodies of his
brothers, nieces, and nephews?

If I visit that far away country today,
will I see his stocky figure-ghost
walking freely through the streets
of Germany, will I feel culpability
hanging, feel grieving in the air, or will I hear
his deep voice saying softly, simply,
*I wanted to live, I wanted to live.*

MAUREEN SHERBONDY

## Pursuing Freedom

Haitians,
hunger, horror,
fear of persecution,
crossing the ocean,
rickety, wooden boat,
sharks, storms,
waves churning,
diseases, deaths,
dodging the Coast Guard,
dry land,
passing children to the shore
like potato sacks,
a rush for freedom.

BRENDA KAY LEDFORD

# Changes

Don't ask me to leave you.
I know their waste is poured
upon your heart.

You have changed—markedly—
during our time together.
I still recognize you—the central force,
and meaningful. This is the stable attraction
I retain and continue with you.

You—you're so brilliant, even
with those who use and abuse
your potential.
Your straight ashen hair is
now curly brown and black.

What once was, isn't—yet the greatness remains.
I still love you.
That which was so young,
now seems so much older.

Yes—you and I have both changed.
But we understand and for this
dear Boston, I do still love you.

TIMOTHY F. CROWLEY

## At Ellis Island

I wander room to room,
photo to photo, seeking a face.

My face.

Could be a man or woman,
old or young, proud, downtrodden,
impassioned, bewildered.

Teenager with torn
leather valises, smiling that
shit-eating grin of the accepted

wide as the Grand Canyon
sizzling in late-afternoon sun.

Old wizener with cigar, staring
at no one but now me.

Three tall Jamaicans
in their prim dresses and high
turbans, would not be
turned away by
any force on earth.

This icon, tasseled shawl, embroidered
towel, bejeweled zither could
by rights belong
to one of us standing

here deciphering,
claiming ourselves the eyes
of now and then.

The great Registry Hall still
gaggles with voices unheard and unknown,
languages our closed eyes bring back,
the same voices quizzical,
intense, this flood of the world

beyond all rocks and chasms,
alighting, roving, waiting

for that new self: new name,
new soil, new light, new isle of peace.

What does it mean to be labeled
disease by disease with chalk,
eyelid by eyelid lifted with a hook,
inspecting, judging each crevice, each surface,
withholding or allowing like a clock?

For dinners sitting around
dusty with real china, embossed,
stepping at last into
a hearing room for pleadings—

Where do we go now?


Stairs of Separation
to steel mills, tool and die,
sweat-shops of a silent drudgery
paid dearly for in bones?

What can these faces tell us?

They knew well what they wanted,
what they left behind,
what hardships make a life

worth living, sacred artifacts
a soul can't do without, dying
to the body of the old.

This is a world of flinting
who we are, knowing the knife-edge
of flesh transported

garbled language
of new time and place

hands clenching all claims,
all frayed belongings,
Bibles, ticket-stubs, razors, shawls—

still in these echoing
human caverns

meet us strangely

face to face.


DAVID RADAVICH

## Tuesday Woman

"Our folks were prejudiced, but consider the Negroes
       they knew,"
             sister said frowning.
I ventured, "But what about Zola?"

Zola who came on Tuesdays to stand on swollen ankles
             sprinkling sheets,
pillows slips, and towels for us to dirty…running
       rivulets of sweat
             as her dark face
sucked up the iron's heat…a hard afternoon's work
             for five dollars.
Zola alone at the kitchen table eating our leftovers…her
       songs and stories
             feeding me the best she had to offer.

Visiting her in that other part of town.
Standing on the porch with mother…talking through
       the screen door.
Smelling tension between them.

Asking, "Why didn't we go inside?"
Learning, "It just isn't done…it isn't proper."

Zola, what did you think about us?

RUTH WINCHESTER WARE, PH.D.

## Two Ways to Leave Home

These photos, relics, words,
they remember the Irish,
the ones who bought passage,
not knowing what *steerage* meant,
knowing only hunger at home
and the Siren's call from Boston.

These innocents packed a bag,
a bundle,
even their own food,
and a crusted cookpot,
then walked into *steerage*
beneath the windy deck.
In that pit, where air was parceled out,
then squeezed from each dole
into soured, rotten juice,
there they learned what *steerage* meant.

And on the day we saw them—
these photos, relics, words,
in the harbor museum at Cobh, Ireland,
the cruise ship Norwegia,
whose pampered guests sat on plump cushions
and drank sweet lemonade,
lolled in the waters just beyond.

BETSY HUMPHREYS

# Wait

    The room is dim
crowded.
Behind clutches of conjoined seating,
cardboard landscapes hang precisely
where windows ought to be,
corner tables littered
with newspapers and month-old magazines.

    A black man in white t-shirt
paces by the Coke machine
distracted
face unreadable in the gloom.
He pivots; (red-tinged) light pans
across his features. Worry
levels his expression
dulls his eyes. His child,
cocoa-sweet girl
still, indifferent
burning dim with fever,
in her mother's arms.

    In the far corner, a woman
hugs her summer-white purse tight
against ample breasts,
decades mapped on swollen legs
by meandering blue highways. Staring
at Letterman on the tube,

blinded by weariness
she rocks back and forth
tuned to an uneasy frequency
revisiting the old man's collapse
too afraid to close her eyes
dreading the summons
to a small room off the hall.

A name is called.
Heads turn, watch.
A hemp-skinned boy,
seeping gash garnished with red bandanna
clean, white this morning by his mother's hand,
rises slowly, muttering Spanish under his breath,
cursing the needle and thread to come
(why not slashing steel that opened his thigh?)

    We all sit, wait,
reading yesterday's headlines,
        wishing it were anytime but now.


PATRICIA W. BARBER

## How Light, the Severed Head

How light, the severed head
of an eyeless bird, peppered
in gentle brown feathers.

The offering of a helpless killer,
a wing of awkward bones, you
tell me it's just nature. Food chains
and natural selection. I cry

for broken things, a single
graying talon, curling
in the brutal sun. Twisted
over on itself like a stomachache.

I want to wrap these things
in parchment, but there is only
white plastic, wires swathed
in cardboard colors, and you,

light as saliva sticky feathers, already watching the tabby
bat at mourning
doves and vanishing time.

E. V. NOECHEL

## Learning English

What is the meaning of this word, Father,
this small one in the middle of the page?
Do I have to look it up in the dictionary?
Can't you this once just tell me
so we can both remain where we are
together in the light Mozart brings
from the beige console, you on the sofa
with your pipe lit and your eyes shut,
me reading on the rug, stuck at a word
so simple it will never be said?

## Lección de inglés

¿Qué quiere decir esta palabra, papá
esta pequeña en el centro de la página?
¿He de ir a buscarla en el diccionario?
¿Sólo esta vez no me la puedes explicar
para que los dos nos podamos quedar
aquí juntos en la luz que Mozart trae
de la consola amarilla, tú en el sofá
con la pipa prendida y los ojos ausentes,
yo en la alfombra leyendo, detenido
por una palabra tan simple que nunca se dirá?

MARK SMITH-SOTO

# Ancestors

Praise for the pirate
who kicks his high boots
through swaying sea oats
to shake sand from his shoes.

Trapped in the dark,
he grabs his stock
to ride a sea pony
along the shore,
a lantern tied
'round the horse's neck.

He works as night fisherman,
trying to lure
a passing vessel
onto a sand bar,
sinking the ship.

Like the pounce of a cat,
he'll rescues sailors abandoning ship.
He'll plunder cinnamon, rice, and silks
sailed from the Orient,
takes tropical fruit,
Persian spices,
tiles from Constantinople,
and if he is blessed by fortune,
Spanish Gold.

He'll risk everything—
his life tilting on this edge,
searching, cheating
for this small vanity.

His life is caught
on Carolina shoals.
He knows being a rescuer
means acquiring spoils.

JOY ACEY

## How Tall Is your Boy?

Asks a round faced native girl
    in Quito.
Cinched on her back is a woven sash
    bright as a rainbow; her son
    peeks with the same sweet face.
Old with experience, she is younger than
    my teenaged son.

A vast distance from her life
    to mine.
I put my hand out, palm down
    above my shoulder,
She laughs, and
    music echoes
in the dark child's eyes.

She explains this hands-down gesture
    is used
for animals and inanimate objects:
    corn plants, piles of laundry
    dogs, and llamas.

She tilts my hand up to show how people
    are measured
in her culture, to show respect,
the hand vertical
    with fingers
reaching toward the sky.

JOY ACEY

## The Naming

Her name is Alana, although she doesn't know it yet.
        She lives in an orphanage
in the province of Hunan, China. In her dark
        shiny eyes are mirrored the assorted hopes
of our family to have a daughter/granddaughter/niece;
        it will be many years before she understands this.
Alana's picture shows her busily chewing on a toy
        and sporting bright red shoes donned
        specifically for the photo. She doesn't know
        her new mother will weep at the sight
of this picture delivered by the Fed Ex man,
        doesn't know she has tracked the package
by computer from Oregon to North Carolina so she
        can be home to receive it and to take a picture
of the startled delivery man. It is her mom's way
        of creating some kind of history for a baby
who was left when she was about two weeks old,
        accompanied by nothing except the desperate,
        unexpressed desire of a parent for a better life
for her child. We are told she was probably born
        on October 26, 2000, and although this is just
        an educated guess, it seems good to us.

It was after all, the Year of the Dragon. It makes her
>   name and birth date equal numerically to an 11,
>   a master number, and we are sure this is no
coincidence. And it is not even miraculous that our
>   chosen name for her, unbeknownst to us, means
>   *from a distant land.*
I turn on the computer again and bring up the email labeled
>   "pictures" in capital letters. I click onto it, and her face
>   emerges, round, framed by wispy black hair, delicate mouth.
>   Alana Xiao Yi, my granddaughter.

BONNIE MICHAEL

## The Lithuanians  CHRISTMAS, 1997

Face down in the foyer, she lies, that statue my brother bought
from the son of a painter our grandparents befriended
before the Second World War. In the afternoon sun,
her bronze back—slightly arched—gleams
and her hair—black and thick as licorice—
as usual guards her features.

Today, on the corner of her pedestal, by her outstretched left hand
sits the box of song books, their covers bearing
merry blue carolers wearing red scarves in the snow.
As the evening progresses, the statue disappears
beneath coats, furs, capes;
an antique top hat slants on her left hip.

They were married in '26, my grandparents, quietly, in Paris:
Both were doctors, but Ruth
was the daughter of a stockyards baron,
and Harry, the son of Samuel Bokvits, a Lithuanian tailor
renamed Bakwin at Ellis Island in '96;
in aught-nine, when Harry was thirteen
and reading in the synagogue on East Eleventh,
Ruth was learning to ride sidesaddle, her brown velvet dress
perfectly sized. Of course it was Paris
where these two exchanged vows.
And afterwards, raw oysters in their stomachs
and drunk on champagne,
doctor and doctor walked the Champs Elysées
and talked of buying art.

And in the '30s, solvent as Marshall Field,
in their brownstone on the upper east side,
they held one supper after another, all the artists they knew
shoveling down roast beef and creamed potatoes,
settling on the sofas as Harry's chamber group played Wagner,
each artist, later, sending on a drawing or sculpture.
Diego Rivera was there, and Calder and finally, Ben Shahn—
a tall man, smudged yet not undignified,
ten years nearer Lithuania, with his eyes on injustice:
Dreyfus, Sacco and Vanzetti, sweatshops and the Depression.
Even so, Harry and he became friends, and soon
two of Shahn's watercolors—the Beach at Fire Island, the Clown
with the red face—hung in the front hall.

The Clown still hangs, in fact,
above the coats piled on the bronze his son made
a half-century later,
but the house is changed now my mother owns it: the walls,
a jumble of paintings and prints,
some she and my father bought in France in the '50s,
after she quit medical school; many more he bought,
filling out his history of Revolutionary music
(soldiers stamping, fifes blaring, drums booming);
and here and there, a lesser work
from Ruth and Harry's collection: Kogan, Rivera, Volti, Derain.
(Gone the Cezannes, Van Goghs, Matisse's Woman in Blue.)

Now, instead of quartets and Grade-A beef,
the table is set with peanut butter sandwiches, buffet style,
and upstairs, with his wife and little boy,
Jonathan Shahn sings "O Holy Night" while, in the foyer,
his lovely sculpture gulps for air.

ANDREA SELCH

# Untitled

My feet feel heavy and awkward in this place.
They grind against the rock and pavement;
they drag across roads and sidewalks
that are strange to me.

My hands are tired here.
They feel like old leather,
stretched and wrinkled and forgotten.
But they still work.

My eyes cannot see
what they could once see.
They are pale and dull now.
And have shed too many tears.

But I am here in this place.
And I will build a home.
I will build new hands.
I will build new feet.
I will build new eyes,
to see this new world.

WILL WHITAKER

# Angel Baby Heaven  *Regards to S.L. Clemens*

I been thinkin' 'bout God's Bright Heaven,
and I knows
in heaven there ain't
no streets of gold
with signs that say "White Only."
And there ain't no notice
on them Pearly Gates
that says, "No Blacks Allowed."
And them Holy Water Fonts—
they splash God's grace on jest everybody.
'Cause in heaven, ain't
no black,
ain't no white—
Everybody jest angel color.

C. PLEASANTS YORK

# Little Bird

Maybe I washed the window too clean.
The little bird saw straight
into the living room and right out
the other side to the sky.
He flew fast like a *pelota,* hit the glass,
fell to the ground and was still.
A drop of blood came out near his long beak.
I picked him up. *Pobrecito.*
He weighed nothing. He did not move.
I wished that I had left the window dirty.

But I want to a good job for Mrs. James.
She is kind to me, tells me to sweep
the patio or trim the bushes
even when they don't need it.
I don't want her to see this dead bird.
It would make her sad.
*De prisa*, I get the garden trowel, dig
a small hole under the Pyracantha,
cover the bird with earth and leaves.
I wipe the window clean again.

Two years ago my mother came to visit.
Mrs. James helped pay for the flight.
She practiced Spanish
with my old sick mother,
both of them laughing.
Later, I could not go
to Guatemala to bury my mother.
My father and brother had been killed.
The same people wanted me
in a shallow grave.

Mrs. James comes outside
with a lunch tray. Tamale pie.
She looks at the windows,
"Good job, Manuelito."
I say, "Thank you, Mom."
She thinks I call her 'Ma'm',
but she is my California mom.
She says she likes to cook for me,
same as she cooked for Mr. James
before he passed away.

We sit down at the patio table.
Something moves under the *Pyracantha*.
It's still alive!
I jump to my feet, telling her
how the little bird hit the window,
how I buried it when I thought it was dead.
I dig it up and brush it off and lay it in her hand.

The little bird blinks
and ruffles its feathers.
Mrs. James says,
"He was only stunned.
I'll keep him safe
until he can fly again."


MARTHA KLOPFER

# Louise

Dear Mother,
So steadfast and faithful,
So religious
Thank you so much,
For showing us the path
We are all on
To return where we came.
As we all get closer to the earth
And further from the sky.

Go in peace,
God bless you,
And we remain.
As you remain in us
And all you touched
And gave birth to.

Remember the Nursing Home Chapel
With its stained glass windows,
Crucifixion cross,
Exit signs, wheelchairs,
Old bodies decaying
With senility?
You told us, "this is the path too."

You breathed in with difficulty,
Struggling to keep us company.
A frail old mother

With her unparalyzed left hand
Touching her ancient face.
As your eyes open to space somewhere
With small grunts and cries,
Your withered, wrinkled flesh sagging
On this once blonde-haired
Lithuanian young beauty.

There you were mom:
Nartautus, Mikulis
Lithuania, Chelsea, Everett,
Florence Street,
All our ancestors.

Such is the way
At 89 years,
As no more can be done
As nature takes its course
For you to return,
Leaving behind
Your six children,
Twelve grandchildren,
And dear relatives and friends.

We stood gazing
With eyes moist
As we waited and feared
That final out-breath.
Ah— breathing out;
You were gone
Over to the other side.
Goodbye dear mother.
You taught us:
I am of the nature to get sick,
I will get sick,
I am of the nature to get old,
I will get old,
I am of the nature to die,
I will die.

How are you and I to be
With the dying?
With the living dead?
With the dead?
With my dead mother?

To be with them,
Be with them
As you would be
With yourself
In the present moment,
With this out-breath.

With an empty self
Open to all things
Connected to all things,
Intimately with the oneness
Of life and death.

We are here together very briefly,
So let us accept reality fully
And take care of one another
      While we can.
Go in peace.
May God be with you.
God Bless you all.


WILLIAM MENZA

# Ode to Horace Mann

Be ashamed to die until you have won some victory for humanity.

Be aware that energy is life, save some for your kids.
Be afraid that our minds are bent by news not books.
Be awed by the healing power of the simple purple cone flower.
Be amazed that after four short years she knows so much.
Be awake before the bombs drop, before the money rules.
Be allowed to live in a town that walks and bikes to work and play.
Be amused by ants and birds, goats and potato fields, sycamores and lilacs.
Be angry only long enough to solve the problem, then move on.
Be ashamed to die until you have won some victory for humanity.

DOUG STUBER

# Pink Chang

Brave children, you don't know how
Your starvation reflects unequal distribution
Of wealth. You don't have the strength
To wonder how much your brothers have.
But now you have the town TV.

Brave parents, you know how much
We have. Your experience says
The sardine boat trip is worth the risk.
Enslaved, but in the land of plenty,
Now you can see it for yourself.

Hard work yields crops from a living rain.
Abide your ancient prayers. But
In this new place, hard work can
Yield these luxuries if you have
The nerve to pull away from

Your enslaver. English helps.
Relatives in some far-off town
Help even more, so good
Luck in your American dream.
Welcome, as they say, to the machine.

DOUG STUBER

## An Alien Dream

I dream of palm fronds and green coconut babies
    strapped to their mother's armpit,
        their arms cowering over the seashore.

I dream of beaches and blue seas,
    of sand married to sun-tan backs,
    of bikinis and fruits-of-the-loom jumping
        into shallow water,
          splashing each other,
            giggling.

I dream
    of ski-boats skidding away to meet Miami Vice heroes,
    of little boys and girls building modern caves offshore.

I dream
    of bicycles and age-tortured buses shuffling for space
        before green lights turn to red.
I dream of men with long dark hair like fur on wet pugs,

    Of game cocks and Chihuahuas and cocker spaniels
        rehearsing for prom night,
    of dandelions flaunting brilliant faces along pavements
        in the evening sun,
    white short-sleeved shirts and khaki pants
        pushing trucks swollen with coconuts
bound for the marketplace.

I dream of wanton faces and hope-littered smiles watching me
when their tired dark pupils find me driving
a Ford Mercury to Managua.


EMMANUEL K. NGWAINMBI

## This Is How

At dawn I hold the lamb for him. First lulled
by warmth, I recoil when the knife opens
its throat, when legs flail, slow, then pulse

against mine. The blood—
sticky on my hands. Bleating turns to moans
turns to silence. *This is how*

*we kill in Zimbabwe.* He shows me how
to retract the head, baring
the throat. *This is how the Hebrews kill*;

*first the artery, then the spinal cord.*
He tells how the killing was done
to his own, how one day soldiers razed his village,

forced him to watch them bind his sister, his only sister—
*lovely as a gazelle, pure as a lamb—*
before coming for him. *This is how*

*you make the cut.* He spreads his fingers
into a V, easing the knife between, separating
skin from abdomen, foreleg from shoulder, careful

that not one bone be broken. His voice—
serene yet resistant. On him
they cut tendons, then other parts. We are into this now,

slicing and pulling, forearm deep in gore, washing
intestines before the heat comes.  I take the blade
in haste, cut deep into the wrong flesh,

my own blood joining
the other.  I press hard until
the bleeding stops, and we work on.

Late morning when the knives
are cleaned, when the lamb has been
prepared for the feast, he asks

for my hand, works in stinging
ointment, says, *This is how
we help the wound to mend.*


FRED BAHNSON

## Ode to an Abandoned Name

Ugly in the mouth, you were
the kind of name tortured
into playground taunts: *Face-Ick! Face-Sick!*
Hung across my brow, a banner
inviting insult: *Hunkie! Polack!*
I hated you without knowing you.
The thin lips of my immigrant grandmother
clamped shut across your meaning.
She died without ever uttering your true
sound. Some bureaucrat called Smith or Miller
with a long line of haunt-eyed gypsies
yet to name, corrupted music imperfectly heard
in impatience. Now on the flickering manifests
conjured from the vaults of Ellis Island
you sprawl, spelled a hundred ways—
*Faszik, Faček, Fahsic, Fassig, Fosicj*—echoing
the whispered sibilants and swallowed finials
of your homeplaces: *Zedelnez, Dubrinice,
Beohew, Chechly, Jusionika*. We were numerous:
*Galician, Slovenian, Ruthenian*, weary emigrants across
the Sudentenland, a tribe of wanderers
slipping past frontiers. From Herzegovina
to Poland you were whispered and written
again and again in whatever letters
came easy to the pen. Finally, on a side street
in steel-town Pennsylvania, came your evolutionary
dead-end. Emma made borscht
and called it beet soup. Made her children
Frank and Fred and Ruth. A stone slab,

immovable even by angels, she blocked
the kitchen doorway, hiding recipes
based on roots. Never singing or speaking
her childhood, she made you too dead
for resurrection. I search the maps in vain:
*Oponice* has vanished under waves of armies;
*Moravia* and *Galicia*, quaint historical oddities,
grace the roach-chewed antique (*Europe 1815–1866*)
scanned into a library database, then discarded.
Likewise, I erased you from my birth certificate,
taking out a genetic line that stretches back across
the Caucasus into India, spitting on a father's
ownership of me. Misspelled and unloved,
you are chiseled now only
on his tombstone, left to tell the tale:
How a thin boy and a stout square-jawed girl
came down the gangplank alone, their names
lost forever the first time they were spoken,
the wind carrying them out the barred windows,
the mouth of the Hudson
swallowing them whole.


JEANNETTE CABANIS-BREWIN

## a ransom of bones

these bones
these bones
touch them gently
for their blackness
have been known
to pick
the locks of
hidden rooms
empty rooms
open doors

I have been this way before
passing as the *exotic foreigner*
denying the color of my
gloved hands
turning away from the dead
incantations of slaves
their voices rising
heaving through my throat
almost telling my secret

oh spirit
blow on me a slave wind
a night of stolen rapture
bleeding my name
from the river
where my blood is born

oh spirit
ritualize the collapse
of a black woman's sap
like the annual flow of the birch
interrupted by
a white man's decision

oh spirit
forgive me for the unfurling of
unfamiliar fabric
in unfamiliar rooms
that forbid morning to enter

i am one locked away
the one paid for
in foreign currency
the currency of deceit

*five hundred pesos a year*

to change the water at
the altar

*five hundred pesos a year*

to remember to forget
a slave mother dying
crying veiled tears

my spirit returns
crossing dark slave thresholds
speaking through muted
smoke before collapsing
beneath my mother's fire

i have lost track of
my secret in this dance
i have lost track
of all other skin i've worn

the calculus of my sins
become sweet whispered drama
for the keepers of the secret

i have swallowed
all the keys
to all the doors
that keep me

oh spirit
touch these bones gently
when they appear
as screams
crossing borders
singing dirges
in familiar
tongues
revenge
sacrifice

i travel
to this myth of home
as transparent as faith
as transparent as the myth
of white face white neck
white arms white thighs
transparent as blue eyes

*five hundred pesos a year*

for the privilege to whisper
but these swallowed keys jingle
threaten to strangle me
with the story of betrayal
the story of a black girl
who walked through
the love light
of her mother's eyes
becoming
the story of a white woman
living on the edges of night

*five hundred pesos a year*
*five hundred pesos a year*

i pay my own skin
for the price of a key
a room a rape a birth

*five hundred pesos a year*
*five hundred pesos a year*
*five hundred pesos a year*

i pay
for this nourishment
this spicy soup of antebellum
i pay to commit these
sins of the tongue

to keep me white
alive locked away
in freedom's dusty
cubicle
locked away
inside someone else's journey

*five hundred pesos a year*

to anoint these bones
with the secrets
i weave to reseal
the lock
protect the unfurling
unfamiliar fabric of memory

*five hundred pesos a year*

to grow old
sit behind gloves
become
the bondsman's daughter
counting the tornadoes
i will unleash
painting my lips
with the colors
of somewhere else

oh spirit
bury these bones
under a forgiving sky
feed them the holiness of sunlight
the holiness of breath

*five hundred pesos a year*
*five hundred pesos a year*

to sharpen my nipples
their language memories
of another freedom
wait for the return of the bondsman

*five hundred pesos a year*

to lock away
what it is
he must never remember
the darkness of my body
offering up questions
he cannot answer
the darkness of words
that spill
all over floors stain chairs

eat into curtains
paint the walls
with the tongue of his seed

*i joyously pay to write these other betrayals*

to kiss memory
back into my bones

these bones
these bones
touch them gently
for they have been known
to dig themselves
into sky under skin
turn light into sharp crystals
walk across fire
turning this denial of blackness
into noose
tight intact
still within reach
breathing
disguised as river
needing
a new ransom


JAKI SHELTON GREEN

## Who Am I, without Exile?

Stranger on the river bank,
like the river, water binds me to your name.
Nothing brings me back from this distance
to the oasis: neither war nor peace.
Nothing grants me entry into the gospels.
Nothing. Nothing shines from the shores
of ebb and flow between the Tigris and the Nile.
Nothing lifts me down from the Pharaoh's chariots.
Nothing carries me, or loads me with an idea:
neither nostalgia, nor promise.
What shall I do? What shall I do without exile
and a long night of gazing at the water?

Water binds me to your name.
Nothing takes me away from the butterflies of dream.
Nothing gives me reality: neither dust, nor fire.
What shall I do without the roses of Samarkand?
What shall I do in a square, where singers are
worn smooth by moonstones?

We have become weightless,
as light as our dwellings in distant winds.
We have, both of us, befriended the strange beings in the
clouds.
We have both been freed from the gravity of the land of
identity.
What shall we do?
What shall we do without exile
and long nights of gazing at the water?

Water binds me to your name.
Nothing is left of me except you.
Nothing is left of you except me—
a stranger caressing the thighs of a stranger.
O stranger, what will we do with what is left
of the stillness and the brief sleep between two myths?
Nothing carries us: neither path nor home.
Was this the same path from the beginning?
Or did our dreams find a Mongolian horse on a hill
and exchange us for him?
What shall we do?
What shall we do without exile?


MAHMOUD DARWISH

## What IS diversity?

*Diversity invites a broader view of the world around us....*

If we shrink the earth's population to a village of precisely 100 people, with all the existing human ratios remaining the same, it will look like the following:

- 57 Asians
- 21 Europeans
- 14 from the Western Hemisphere (both north and south)
- 52 would be female
- 48 would be male
- 70 would be non-white, 30 would be white
- 70 would be non-Christian, 30 would be Christian
- 89 would be heterosexual, 11 would be homosexual
- 6 people, all from the US, would possess 59% of the entire world's wealth
- 50 would suffer from malnutrition
- 70 would be unable to read
- 80 would live in substandard housing
- 1 would have a college education
- 1 would own a computer
- 1 would be near death, one would be near birth

*When one considers our world from such a compressed perspective, the need for acceptance, understanding and education becomes glaringly apparent.*

AUTHOR AND SOURCE UNKNOWN